The Rite Words

A Notebook for Mass

THE RITE WORDS

A NOTEBOOK FOR MASS

by

ROBYN C. BROYLES

SPARKITECT MEDIA

The Sparkitect Media name and logo are trademarks of Sparkitect Media.
http://www.sparkitectmedia.com

THE RITE WORDS: A NOTEBOOK FOR MASS

Published by Sparkitect Media, Houston, Texas. Printing information for this book is found on the last page.

Book design and cover design by Robyn C. Broyles.

ISBN-10: 0692494421

ISBN-13: 978-0692494424

A.M.D.G.

For the members of

St. Ignatius Loyola Catholic Church

in Spring, Texas,
and in particular for our dedicated pastor,

Father Norbert Maduzia Jr., E.V., D.Min.,

who tends his flock
with faith and perseverence.
There is no community
with whom I would rather share
my Mass experience on earth.

Do not absent yourself from your own assemblies,
as some do, but encourage each other;
the more so as you see the Day drawing near.
—*Hebrews 10:25, NJB*

How to Use This Book

The Rite Words is a journal for Catholic Mass. It is meant to support you as you pray with the liturgy and listen to God's Word. The Mass is "the primary and indispensable source from which the faithful are to derive the true Christian spirit",[1] and this book will help you take even greater advantage of the graces you receive from it. It can be used for weekly or daily Mass. Use it as much or as little as you like, according to what benefits your spiritual life.

This journal is divided into two main parts. The *Mass Notes* part is a tool you can use to keep a record of meaningful passages from the readings, interesting phrases from the Collect and other Mass prayers, and helpful nuggets from the homily. These are the words the

---

1. *Sacrosanctum Concilium* (*Constitution on the Sacred Liturgy*) (*SC*), 14.

Holy Spirit is calling to your attention. By writing them on paper, you are taking the first step to writing them on your heart.[2] Later, you can reread them for inspiration, transfer them to another prayer journal, or even use them when sharing the faith with someone else.

This section is mainly for use during the Liturgy of the Word. It is long enough for about a year's worth of Sunday and Holy Day Masses. At the Liturgy of the Eucharist, it's better put the *Mass Notes* away and focus on the presence of Jesus Christ on the altar.

Mass Notes is made up of two–page spreads and has areas to record the details of the liturgy you are attending, such as the specific celebration (for example, "Second Sunday of Lent" or "Solemnity of the Immaculate Conception") and the date. Plenty of blank lines are provided for you to make notes on Liturgy of the Word. Since a key part of our prayer at Mass is the Prayer of the Faithful, there is also a special place for recording these prayer intentions so you can make them your own. As you pray daily, these public petitions can help you orient your prayer to the Mass, since "[p]rayer internalizes and assimilates the liturgy during and after its celebration."[3] Fill in only what is helpful to you; don't feel obligated to write something in every blank.

2. See Deuteronomy 11:18.
3. *SC* 14.

The second part, *Prayers*, is meant to help you enter more deeply into prayer, both while at Mass and after it is over. Every member of the Church is called to "full and active participation" at Mass.[4] This participation starts with uniting our prayer to the prayer and sacrifice of Jesus made present on the altar.

The *Prayer* part is divided into three sections. *Intentions* is a place for you to list those people and hopes you wish to pray for regularly while at Mass, especially after Communion. *Devotions* is there for you to record, in your own words, the prayers you offer to God. When you read these written prayers again later, they become an interior form of *vocal prayer*, which "follow[s] Christ's example of praying to his Father and teaching the Our Father to his disciples."[5] Use *Resolutions* to record what you hear the Holy Spirit sending you to do once you leave Mass.

4. *Catechism of the Catholic Church* (CCC), paragraph 2655.

5. *CCC* 2722.

Mass Notes

*[T]he words that I have spoken
to you are spirit and life.*
—John 6:63b, RSV-CE

Celebration _____

Church _____ Date _____

Presider _____

Homilist _____

Readings _____

Readings and Homily Notes

_____
_____
_____
_____
_____
_____
_____
_____
_____
_____
_____
_____
_____
_____
_____
_____
_____
_____
_____
_____

Prayer of the Faithful

For...

℣. Let us pray to the Lord.   ℞. Lord, hear our prayer.

Mass Notes

[T]he words that I have spoken
to you are spirit and life.
—John 6:63b, RSV-CE

Celebration _____

Church _____ Date _____

Presider _____

Homilist _____

Readings _____

Readings and Homily Notes

Prayer of the Faithful

For...

℣. Let us pray to the Lord.   ℟. Lord, hear our prayer.

Mass Notes

*[T]he words that I have spoken
to you are spirit and life.*
—John 6:63b, RSV-CE

Celebration _____

Church _____ Date _____

Presider _____

Homilist _____

Readings _____

Readings and Homily Notes

Prayer of the Faithful

For...

℣. Let us pray to the Lord.   ℟. Lord, hear our prayer.

Mass Notes

*[T]he words that I have spoken
to you are spirit and life.*
—John 6:63b, RSV-CE

Celebration _____

Church _____ Date _____

Presider _____

Homilist _____

Readings _____

Readings and Homily Notes

Prayer of the Faithful

For...

℣. Let us pray to the Lord.   ℟. Lord, hear our prayer.

Mass Notes

Celebration _____

Church _____ Date _____

Presider _____

Homilist _____

Readings _____

Readings and Homily Notes

_____
_____
_____
_____
_____
_____
_____
_____
_____
_____
_____
_____
_____
_____
_____
_____
_____
_____
_____
_____
_____
_____
_____

Prayer of the Faithful

For...

℣. Let us pray to the Lord.   ℟. Lord, hear our prayer.

Mass Notes

[T]he words that I have spoken to you are spirit and life.
—John 6:63b, RSV-CE

Celebration _____

Church _____ Date _____

Presider _____

Homilist _____

Readings _____

Readings and Homily Notes

Prayer of the Faithful

For...

℣. Let us pray to the Lord.　　　℟. Lord, hear our prayer.

Mass Notes

*[T]he words that I have spoken
to you are spirit and life.*
—*John 6:63b, RSV-CE*

Celebration _____

Church _____ Date _____

Presider _____

Homilist _____

Readings _____

Readings and Homily Notes

_____

_____

_____

_____

_____

_____

_____

_____

_____

_____

_____

_____

_____

_____

_____

_____

_____

_____

_____

_____

Prayer of the Faithful

For...

℣. Let us pray to the Lord.   ℟. Lord, hear our prayer.

Mass Notes

[T]he words that I have spoken to you are spirit and life.
—*John 6:63b, RSV-CE*

Celebration _____

Church _____ Date _____

Presider _____

Homilist _____

Readings _____

Readings and Homily Notes

_____

_____

_____

_____

_____

_____

_____

_____

_____

_____

_____

_____

_____

_____

_____

_____

_____

_____

_____

_____

Prayer of the Faithful

For...

℣. Let us pray to the Lord.   ℟. Lord, hear our prayer.

Mass Notes

Celebration _____

Church _____ Date _____

Presider _____

Homilist _____

Readings _____

Readings and Homily Notes

_____
_____
_____
_____
_____
_____
_____
_____
_____
_____
_____
_____
_____
_____
_____
_____
_____
_____
_____
_____

Prayer of the Faithful

For...

℣. Let us pray to the Lord.   ℟. Lord, hear our prayer.

Mass Notes

*[T]he words that I have spoken
to you are spirit and life.*
—John 6:63b, RSV-CE

Celebration _____

Church _____ Date _____

Presider _____

Homilist _____

Readings _____

Readings and Homily Notes

Prayer of the Faithful

For...

℣. Let us pray to the Lord.   ℟. Lord, hear our prayer.

Mass Notes

Celebration _____

Church _____ Date _____

Presider _____

Homilist _____

Readings _____

Readings and Homily Notes

_____
_____
_____
_____
_____
_____
_____
_____
_____
_____
_____
_____
_____
_____
_____
_____
_____
_____
_____
_____
_____
_____
_____

Prayer of the Faithful

For...

℣. Let us pray to the Lord.   ℟. Lord, hear our prayer.

Mass Notes

*[T]he words that I have spoken
to you are spirit and life.*
—John 6:63b, RSV-CE

Celebration _____

Church _____ Date _____

Presider _____

Homilist _____

Readings _____

Readings and Homily Notes

_____

_____

_____

_____

_____

_____

_____

_____

_____

_____

_____

_____

_____

_____

_____

_____

_____

_____

_____

_____

_____

_____

Prayer of the Faithful

For...

℣. Let us pray to the Lord.   ℟. Lord, hear our prayer.

Mass Notes

*[T]he words that I have spoken
to you are spirit and life.*
—John 6:63b, RSV-CE

Celebration _____

Church _____ Date _____

Presider _____

Homilist _____

Readings _____

Readings and Homily Notes

Prayer of the Faithful

For...

℣. Let us pray to the Lord.   ℟. Lord, hear our prayer.

Mass Notes

*[T]he words that I have spoken
to you are spirit and life.*
—John 6:63b, RSV-CE

Celebration _____

Church _____ Date _____

Presider _____

Homilist _____

Readings _____

Readings and Homily Notes

Prayer of the Faithful

For...

℣. Let us pray to the Lord. ℟. Lord, hear our prayer.

Mass Notes

[T]he words that I have spoken to you are spirit and life.
—John 6:63b, RSV-CE

Celebration _____

Church _____ Date _____

Presider _____

Homilist _____

Readings _____

Readings and Homily Notes

Prayer of the Faithful

For...

℣. Let us pray to the Lord.   ℟. Lord, hear our prayer.

Mass Notes

*[T]he words that I have spoken
to you are spirit and life.*
—John 6:63b, RSV-CE

Celebration _____

Church _____ Date _____

Presider _____

Homilist _____

Readings _____

Readings and Homily Notes

Prayer of the Faithful

For...

℣. Let us pray to the Lord.   ℟. Lord, hear our prayer.

Mass Notes

[T]he words that I have spoken to you are spirit and life.
—John 6:63b, RSV-CE

Celebration _____

Church _____ Date _____

Presider _____

Homilist _____

Readings _____

Readings and Homily Notes

_____
_____
_____
_____
_____
_____
_____
_____
_____
_____
_____
_____
_____
_____
_____
_____
_____
_____
_____
_____
_____
_____
_____
_____

Prayer of the Faithful

For...

℣. Let us pray to the Lord.   ℟. Lord, hear our prayer.

Mass Notes

Celebration _____

Church _____ Date _____

Presider _____

Homilist _____

Readings _____

Readings and Homily Notes

_____
_____
_____
_____
_____
_____
_____
_____
_____
_____
_____
_____
_____
_____
_____
_____
_____
_____
_____
_____
_____
_____
_____

Prayer of the Faithful

For...

℣. Let us pray to the Lord.   ℟. Lord, hear our prayer.

Mass Notes

[T]he words that I have spoken to you are spirit and life.
—John 6:63b, RSV-CE

Celebration _____

Church _____ Date _____

Presider _____

Homilist _____

Readings _____

Readings and Homily Notes

_____

_____

_____

_____

_____

_____

_____

_____

_____

_____

_____

_____

_____

_____

_____

_____

_____

_____

_____

_____

_____

_____

_____

_____

Prayer of the Faithful

For...

℣. Let us pray to the Lord.   ℟. Lord, hear our prayer.

Mass Notes

Celebration _____

Church _____ Date _____

Presider _____

Homilist _____

Readings _____

Readings and Homily Notes

Prayer of the Faithful

For...

℣. Let us pray to the Lord.   ℟. Lord, hear our prayer.

Mass Notes

*[T]he words that I have spoken
to you are spirit and life.*
—John 6:63b, RSV-CE

Celebration _____

Church _____ Date _____

Presider _____

Homilist _____

Readings _____

Readings and Homily Notes

_____
_____
_____
_____
_____
_____
_____
_____
_____
_____
_____
_____
_____
_____
_____
_____
_____
_____
_____
_____
_____
_____
_____

Prayer of the Faithful

For...

℣. Let us pray to the Lord.   ℟. Lord, hear our prayer.

Mass Notes

[T]he words that I have spoken to you are spirit and life.
—John 6:63b, RSV-CE

Celebration _____

Church _____ Date _____

Presider _____

Homilist _____

Readings _____

Readings and Homily Notes

_____

_____

_____

_____

_____

_____

_____

_____

_____

_____

_____

_____

_____

_____

_____

_____

_____

_____

_____

_____

_____

Prayer of the Faithful

For...

℣. Let us pray to the Lord.   ℟. Lord, hear our prayer.

Mass Notes

[T]he words that I have spoken
to you are spirit and life.
—John 6:63b, RSV-CE

Celebration _____

Church _____ Date _____

Presider _____

Homilist _____

Readings _____

Readings and Homily Notes

Prayer of the Faithful

For...

℣. Let us pray to the Lord.   ℟. Lord, hear our prayer.

Mass Notes

[T]he words that I have spoken to you are spirit and life.
—John 6:63b, RSV-CE

Celebration _____

Church _____ Date _____

Presider _____

Homilist _____

Readings _____

Readings and Homily Notes

Prayer of the Faithful

For...

℣. Let us pray to the Lord.   ℟. Lord, hear our prayer.

Mass Notes

*[T]he words that I have spoken
to you are spirit and life.*
—John 6:63b, RSV-CE

Celebration _____

Church _____   Date _____

Presider _____

Homilist _____

Readings _____

Readings and Homily Notes

Prayer of the Faithful

For...

℣. Let us pray to the Lord.   ℟. Lord, hear our prayer.

Mass Notes

[T]he words that I have spoken
to you are spirit and life.
—*John 6:63b, RSV-CE*

Celebration _____

Church _____ Date _____

Presider _____

Homilist _____

Readings _____

Readings and Homily Notes

Prayer of the Faithful

For...

℣. Let us pray to the Lord.   ℟. Lord, hear our prayer.

Mass Notes

*[T]he words that I have spoken
to you are spirit and life.*
—John 6:63b, RSV-CE

Celebration _____

Church _____ Date _____

Presider _____

Homilist _____

Readings _____

Readings and Homily Notes

Prayer of the Faithful

For...

℣. Let us pray to the Lord.   ℟. Lord, hear our prayer.

Mass Notes

[T]he words that I have spoken
to you are spirit and life.
—John 6:63b, RSV-CE

Celebration _____

Church _____ Date _____

Presider _____

Homilist _____

Readings _____

Readings and Homily Notes

Prayer of the Faithful

For...

℣. Let us pray to the Lord.   ℟. Lord, hear our prayer.

Mass Notes

*[T]he words that I have spoken
to you are spirit and life.*
—John 6:63b, RSV-CE

Celebration _____

Church _____ Date _____

Presider _____

Homilist _____

Readings _____

Readings and Homily Notes

_____

_____

_____

_____

_____

_____

_____

_____

_____

_____

_____

_____

_____

_____

_____

_____

_____

_____

_____

_____

_____

_____

Prayer of the Faithful

For...

℣. Let us pray to the Lord.   ℟. Lord, hear our prayer.

Mass Notes

Celebration _____

Church _____ Date _____

Presider _____

Homilist _____

Readings _____

Readings and Homily Notes

_____

_____

_____

_____

_____

_____

_____

_____

_____

_____

_____

_____

_____

_____

_____

_____

_____

_____

_____

_____

_____

_____

Prayer of the Faithful

For...

℣. Let us pray to the Lord.   ℟. Lord, hear our prayer.

Mass Notes

*[T]he words that I have spoken
to you are spirit and life.*
—John 6:63b, RSV-CE

Celebration _____

Church _____ Date _____

Presider _____

Homilist _____

Readings _____

Readings and Homily Notes

Prayer of the Faithful

For...

℣. Let us pray to the Lord.   ℟. Lord, hear our prayer.

Mass Notes

[T]he words that I have spoken to you are spirit and life.
—John 6:63b, RSV-CE

Celebration _____

Church _____ Date _____

Presider _____

Homilist _____

Readings _____

Readings and Homily Notes

Prayer of the Faithful

For...

℣. Let us pray to the Lord.   ℟. Lord, hear our prayer.

Mass Notes

[T]he words that I have spoken
to you are spirit and life.
—John 6:63b, RSV-CE

Celebration _____

Church _____ Date _____

Presider _____

Homilist _____

Readings _____

Readings and Homily Notes

Prayer of the Faithful

For...

℣. Let us pray to the Lord.   ℟. Lord, hear our prayer.

Mass Notes

*[T]he words that I have spoken
to you are spirit and life.
—John 6:63b, RSV-CE*

Celebration _____

Church _____ Date _____

Presider _____

Homilist _____

Readings _____

Readings and Homily Notes

_____

_____

_____

_____

_____

_____

_____

_____

_____

_____

_____

_____

_____

_____

_____

_____

_____

_____

_____

_____

_____

_____

_____

Prayer of the Faithful

For...

℣. Let us pray to the Lord. ℟. Lord, hear our prayer.

Mass Notes

[T]he words that I have spoken
to you are spirit and life.
—John 6:63b, RSV-CE

Celebration _____

Church _____ Date _____

Presider _____

Homilist _____

Readings _____

Readings and Homily Notes

_____
_____
_____
_____
_____
_____
_____
_____
_____
_____
_____
_____
_____
_____
_____
_____
_____
_____
_____
_____
_____
_____
_____

Prayer of the Faithful

For...

℣. Let us pray to the Lord.   ℟. Lord, hear our prayer.

Mass Notes

*[T]he words that I have spoken
to you are spirit and life.*
—John 6:63b, RSV-CE

Celebration _____

Church _____ Date _____

Presider _____

Homilist _____

Readings _____

Readings and Homily Notes

Prayer of the Faithful

For... _____

_____

_____

_____

_____

_____

_____

℣. Let us pray to the Lord.   ℟. Lord, hear our prayer.

Mass Notes

Celebration ....

Church .... Date ....

Presider ....

Homilist ....

Readings ....

Readings and Homily Notes

_____

_____

_____

_____

_____

_____

_____

_____

_____

_____

_____

_____

_____

_____

_____

_____

_____

_____

_____

Prayer of the Faithful

For... _____

_____

_____

_____

_____

_____

_____

℣. Let us pray to the Lord.　　　℟. Lord, hear our prayer.

Mass Notes

[T]he words that I have spoken to you are spirit and life.
—John 6:63b, RSV-CE

Celebration ....

Church .... Date ....

Presider ....

Homilist ....

Readings ....

Readings and Homily Notes

_____

_____

_____

_____

_____

_____

_____

_____

_____

_____

_____

_____

_____

_____

_____

_____

_____

_____

_____

_____

Prayer of the Faithful

For... _____

℣. Let us pray to the Lord.   ℟. Lord, hear our prayer.

Mass Notes

*[T]he words that I have spoken
to you are spirit and life.*
—John 6:63b, RSV-CE

Celebration _____

Church _____ Date _____

Presider _____

Homilist _____

Readings _____

Readings and Homily Notes

Prayer of the Faithful

For... _____

_____

_____

_____

_____

_____

℣. Let us pray to the Lord.   ℟. Lord, hear our prayer.

Mass Notes

[T]he words that I have spoken
to you are spirit and life.
—John 6:63b, RSV-CE

Celebration _____

Church _____ Date _____

Presider _____

Homilist _____

Readings _____

Readings and Homily Notes

Prayer of the Faithful

For... _____

_____

_____

_____

_____

_____

_____

℣. Let us pray to the Lord. ℟. Lord, hear our prayer.

Mass Notes

Celebration ....

Church ....   Date ....

Presider ....

Homilist ....

Readings ....

Readings and Homily Notes

_____

_____

_____

_____

_____

_____

_____

_____

_____

_____

_____

_____

_____

_____

_____

_____

_____

_____

_____

Prayer of the Faithful

For... _____

_____

_____

_____

_____

_____

_____

℣. Let us pray to the Lord.   ℟. Lord, hear our prayer.

Mass Notes

[T]he words that I have spoken
to you are spirit and life.
—John 6:63b, RSV-CE

Celebration _____

Church _____ Date _____

Presider _____

Homilist _____

Readings _____

Readings and Homily Notes

Prayer of the Faithful

For... _____

℣. Let us pray to the Lord.   ℟. Lord, hear our prayer.

Mass Notes

Celebration ....

Church .... Date ....

Presider ....

Homilist ....

Readings ....

Readings and Homily Notes

Prayer of the Faithful

For... _____

_____

_____

_____

_____

_____

_____

℣. Let us pray to the Lord.   ℟. Lord, hear our prayer.

Mass Notes

Celebration ....

Church .... Date ....

Presider ....

Homilist ....

Readings ....

Readings and Homily Notes

Prayer of the Faithful

For... _____

_____

_____

_____

_____

_____

℣. Let us pray to the Lord.   ℟. Lord, hear our prayer.

Mass Notes

*[T]he words that I have spoken
to you are spirit and life.*
—John 6:63b, RSV-CE

Celebration ....

Church .... Date ....

Presider ....

Homilist ....

Readings ....

Readings and Homily Notes

Prayer of the Faithful

For... _____

_____

_____

_____

_____

_____

_____

℣. Let us pray to the Lord.   ℟. Lord, hear our prayer.

Mass Notes

[T]he words that I have spoken to you are spirit and life.
—John 6:63b, RSV-CE

Celebration ....

Church .... Date ....

Presider ....

Homilist ....

Readings ....

Readings and Homily Notes

Prayer of the Faithful

For... _____

_____

_____

_____

_____

_____

_____

℣. Let us pray to the Lord.　　℟. Lord, hear our prayer.

Mass Notes

*[T]he words that I have spoken
to you are spirit and life.*
—John 6:63b, RSV-CE

Celebration

Church .... Date

Presider

Homilist

Readings

Readings and Homily Notes

Prayer of the Faithful

For... _____

_____

_____

_____

_____

_____

℣. Let us pray to the Lord.   ℟. Lord, hear our prayer.

Mass Notes

*[T]he words that I have spoken
to you are spirit and life.*
—John 6:63b, RSV-CE

Celebration ....

Church .... Date ....

Presider ....

Homilist ....

Readings ....

Readings and Homily Notes

Prayer of the Faithful

For...

℣. Let us pray to the Lord.   ℟. Lord, hear our prayer.

Mass Notes

Celebration ....

Church .... Date ....

Presider ....

Homilist ....

Readings ....

Readings and Homily Notes

Prayer of the Faithful

For... _____

_____

_____

_____

_____

_____

℣. Let us pray to the Lord.   ℟. Lord, hear our prayer.

Mass Notes

*[T]he words that I have spoken
to you are spirit and life.*
—John 6:63b, RSV-CE

Celebration ....

Church .... Date ....

Presider ....

Homilist ....

Readings ....

Readings and Homily Notes

Prayer of the Faithful

For... _____

_____

_____

_____

_____

_____

℣. Let us pray to the Lord.   ℟. Lord, hear our prayer.

Mass Notes

Celebration ....

Church .... Date ....

Presider ....

Homilist ....

Readings ....

Readings and Homily Notes

Prayer of the Faithful

For... _____

_____

_____

_____

_____

_____

℣. Let us pray to the Lord.   ℟. Lord, hear our prayer.

Mass Notes

*[T]he words that I have spoken
to you are spirit and life.*
—*John 6:63b, RSV-CE*

Celebration ....

Church .... Date ....

Presider ....

Homilist ....

Readings ....

Readings and Homily Notes

Prayer of the Faithful

For...

℣. Let us pray to the Lord.   ℟. Lord, hear our prayer.

Mass Notes

*[T]he words that I have spoken
to you are spirit and life.*
—John 6:63b, RSV-CE

Celebration _____

Church _____ Date _____

Presider _____

Homilist _____

Readings _____

Readings and Homily Notes

Prayer of the Faithful

For... _____

_____

_____

_____

_____

_____

_____

℣. Let us pray to the Lord.   ℟. Lord, hear our prayer.

Mass Notes

*[T]he words that I have spoken
to you are spirit and life.*
—John 6:63b, RSV-CE

Celebration ....

Church .... Date ....

Presider ....

Homilist ....

Readings ....

Readings and Homily Notes

Prayer of the Faithful

For...

℣. Let us pray to the Lord.   ℟. Lord, hear our prayer.

Mass Notes

[T]he words that I have spoken to you are spirit and life.
—John 6:63b, RSV-CE

Celebration ....

Church .... Date ....

Presider ....

Homilist ....

Readings ....

Readings and Homily Notes

Prayer of the Faithful

For... _____

℣. Let us pray to the Lord.   ℟. Lord, hear our prayer.

Mass Notes

[T]he words that I have spoken
to you are spirit and life.
—John 6:63b, RSV-CE

Celebration _____

Church _____ Date _____

Presider _____

Homilist _____

Readings _____

Readings and Homily Notes

Prayer of the Faithful

For... _____

℣. Let us pray to the Lord.   ℟. Lord, hear our prayer.

Mass Notes

*[T]he words that I have spoken
to you are spirit and life.*
—John 6:63b, RSV-CE

Celebration ....

Church ....   Date ....

Presider ....

Homilist ....

Readings ....

Readings and Homily Notes

_____

_____

_____

_____

_____

_____

_____

_____

_____

_____

_____

_____

_____

_____

Prayer of the Faithful

For... _____

_____

_____

_____

_____

_____

_____

℣. Let us pray to the Lord.   ℟. Lord, hear our prayer.

Prayers

I urge then, first of all that petitions, prayers,
intercessions and thanksgiving
should be offered for everyone.
—1 Timothy 2:1, NJB

(Here list those people and causes for whom you wish to pray at Mass and after Holy Communion.)

Intentions

_____

_____

_____

_____

_____

_____

_____

_____

_____

_____

_____

_____

_____

_____

_____

_____

_____

_____

_____

Prayers

I urge then, first of all that petitions, prayers, intercessions and thanksgiving should be offered for everyone.

—1 Timothy 2:1, NJB

Intentions

Prayers

I urge then, first of all that petitions, prayers,
intercessions and thanksgiving
should be offered for everyone.
—1 Timothy 2:1, NJB

(Here list those people and causes for whom you wish to pray at Mass and after Holy Communion.)

Intentions

Prayers

I urge then, first of all that petitions, prayers,
intercessions and thanksgiving
should be offered for everyone.
—1 Timothy 2:1, NJB

(Here list those people and causes for whom you wish to pray at Mass and after Holy Communion.)

Intentions

_____

_____

_____

_____

_____

_____

_____

_____

_____

_____

_____

_____

_____

_____

_____

_____

_____

_____

_____

_____

_____

Prayers

I urge then, first of all that petitions, prayers,
intercessions and thanksgiving
should be offered for everyone.
—1 Timothy 2:1, NJB

Prayers

[F]or we do not know how to pray as we ought,
but the Spirit himself intercedes for us
with sighs too deep for words.
—Romans 8:26b, RSV-CE

(Here write words of praise and thanksgiving to Our Lord, as well as meditations that come to you at Mass.)

Devotions

Prayers

*[F]or we do not know how to pray as we ought,
but the Spirit himself intercedes for us
with sighs too deep for words.*

—Romans 8:26b, RSV-CE

Devotions

Prayers

*[F]or we do not know how to pray as we ought,
but the Spirit himself intercedes for us
with sighs too deep for words.*

—Romans 8:26b, RSV-CE

(Here write words of praise and thanksgiving to Our Lord, as well as meditations that come to you at Mass.)

Devotions

Prayers

*[F]or we do not know how to pray as we ought,
but the Spirit himself intercedes for us
with sighs too deep for words.*

—Romans 8:26b, RSV-CE

(Here write words of praise and thanksgiving to Our Lord, as well as meditations that come to you at Mass.)

Devotions

Prayers

*[F]or we do not know how to pray as we ought,
but the Spirit himself intercedes for us
with sighs too deep for words.*

—Romans 8:26b, RSV-CE

(Here write words of praise and thanksgiving to Our Lord, as well as meditations that come to you at Mass.)

Devotions

Prayers

By this is my Father glorified,
that you bear much fruit
and become my disciples.
—John 15:8, NAB-RE

Resolutions

Prayers

By this is my Father glorified,
that you bear much fruit
and become my disciples.
—John 15:8, NAB-RE

Resolutions

Prayers

By this is my Father glorified,
that you bear much fruit
and become my disciples.
—John 15:8, NAB-RE

*(Here record the actions you hear
the Holy Spirit prompting you to do
in order to build up the Kingdom of God.)*

Resolutions

Prayers

By this is my Father glorified,
that you bear much fruit
and become my disciples.
—John 15:8, NAB-RE

Prayers

*By this is my Father glorified,
that you bear much fruit
and become my disciples.*
—John 15:8, NAB-RE

*(Here record the actions you hear
the Holy Spirit prompting you to do
in order to build up the Kingdom of God.)*

Resolutions

A Note on the Typography

The text of this book is set in Gentium Book Basic, designed by Victor Gaultney. Titles and section headings are set in Asul, designed by Mariela Monsalve. Calligraphic titles are set in Almendra Italic, designed by Ana Sanfelippo. URLs are set in PT Mono Regular, designed by ParaType, Inc.

The symbols for "versicle" and "response" (℣ and ℟, respectively) are glyphs developed by the publisher especially for this work. They are based on the Gentium Book Basic Regular glyphs V and R, respectively, according to the terms of the SIL Open Font License (http://scripts.sil.org/OFL).

The book's pages were laid out and typeset using the open-source application Scribus. More information can be found at the Scribus site (http://www.scribus.net).

The publisher would like to thank those who contributed to the open-source software and fonts used to produce this work.

Made in the USA
Lexington, KY
05 March 2018